30 MINUTE MEALS

igloobooks

Published in 2016
by Igloo Books Ltd
Cottage Farm
Sywell
NN6 0BJ
www.igloobooks.com

Food photography and recipe development:
© Stockfood, The Food Media Agency
Cover image © Stockfood, The Food Media Agency

HUN001 0216
2 4 6 8 10 9 7 5 3 1
ISBN 978-1-78557-530-3

Cover designed by Nicholas Gage
Interiors designed by Charles Wood-Penn
Edited by Caroline Icke

Printed and manufactured in China

Contents

Breakfasts

Pancakes with Bacon and Eggs

SERVES **2**

PREPARATION TIME **5 MINUTES**

COOKING TIME **25 MINUTES**

INGREDIENTS

250 g / 9 oz / 1 ⅔ cups plain (all-purpose) flour
2 tsp baking powder
4 large eggs
300 ml / 10 ½ fl. oz / 1 ¼ cups milk
2 tbsp butter
2 rashers smoked streaky bacon

METHOD

1. Mix the flour and baking powder in a bowl and make a well in the centre. Break in 2 eggs and pour in the milk, then use a whisk to gradually incorporate all of the flour from round the outside.

2. Melt the butter in a small frying pan, then whisk it into the batter. Put the buttered frying pan back over a low heat. You will need 1 tbsp of batter for each pancake and you should be able to cook four pancakes at a time in the frying pan.

3. Spoon the batter into the pan and cook for 2 minutes or until small bubbles start to appear on the surface. Turn the pancakes over with a spatula and cook the other side until golden brown and cooked through.

4. Repeat until all the batter has been used, keeping the finished batches warm in a low oven.

5. Fry the remaining eggs and the bacon in a separate frying pan until the bacon is crisp and the egg whites have set.

6. Divide the pancakes between two warm plates and top with the eggs and bacon.

TOP TIP
Fold a handful of chopped spinach through the batter before cooking.

Scrambled Egg with Asparagus

SERVES 4

PREPARATION TIME 2 MINUTES

COOKING TIME 5 MINUTES

INGREDIENTS

asparagus spears, cut into short lengths
large eggs
bsp butter
inch of salt

METHOD

1. Steam the asparagus for 4 minutes or until tender.

2. Meanwhile, gently beat the eggs with a little salt and pepper to break up the yolks.

3. Heat the butter in a non-stick frying pan until sizzling, then pour in the eggs. Cook over a low heat, stirring constantly until the eggs scramble.

4. Stir in the asparagus and divide between four warm bowls. Serve immediately.

TOP TIP

Great for brunch if you don't have time for breakfast.

Fruity Cereal

METHOD

1. Mix the cereal, dried apple, strawberries and grapes together in a bowl.
2. Pour over the apple juice and serve immediately.

SERVES 1

PREPARATION TIME 5 MINUTES

INGREDIENTS

15 g / ½ oz / ½ cup cereal flakes
2 tbsp dried apple pieces
3 strawberries, quartered
6 green grapes, halved
150 ml / 5 ½ fl. oz / ⅔ cup apple juice

TOP TIP
Sprinkle over 2 tbsp of crunchy granola for extra texture.

Poached Eggs on Toast with Ham and Asparagus

METHOD

1. Steam the asparagus for 5 minutes or until tender.

2. Meanwhile, bring a wide saucepan of water to a gentle simmer and stir in the vinegar.

3. Crack each egg into a cup and pour them smoothly into the water, one at a time. Poach gently for 3 minutes.

4. Toast the bread lightly, then spread with the butter and top with the asparagus and ham. Lay a poached egg on top of each one and serve immediately.

SERVES 4

PREPARATION TIME 10 MINUTES

COOKING TIME 5 MINUTES

INGREDIENTS

asparagus spears, trimmed
tbsp white wine vinegar
large very fresh eggs
slices white bread
tbsp butter
slices honey roast ham

TOP TIP
Try replacing the asparagus with purple sprouting broccoli.

15

Banana and Cinnamon French Toast

SERVES 4

PREPARATION TIME 10 MINUTES

COOKING TIME 6 MINUTES

INGREDIENTS

2 large eggs
75 ml / 2 ½ fl. oz / ⅓ cup whole milk
4 tbsp butter
4 thick slices sourdough bread
3 tbsp dark brown sugar
½ tsp ground cinnamon
2 bananas, sliced
cinnamon sticks to garnish

METHOD

1. Preheat the grill to its highest setting. Lightly beat the eggs with the milk in a wide, shallow dish. Heat half of the butter in a large frying pan until sizzling.

2. Dip the sourdough slices in the egg mixture on both sides until evenly coated, then fry them in the butter for 2 minutes on each side or until golden brown.

3. Meanwhile, gently heat the rest of the butter with the brown sugar and ground cinnamon in a small saucepan to melt the sugar.

4. Transfer the French toast to a grill tray and top with the sliced bananas. Spoon over the brown sugar mixture and top each one with a cinnamon stick, then cook under the grill for 1–2 minutes to caramelize the top.

TOP TIP

Scatter over some honey-roasted almonds for added crunch.

Bacon and Herb Omelette

SERVES 1

PREPARATION TIME 2 MINUTES

COOKING TIME 6 MINUTES

INGREDIENTS

tbsp butter

rasher unsmoked back bacon, chopped

large eggs

tbsp flat leaf parsley, chopped

salt and black pepper

METHOD

1. Heat the butter in a frying pan, then fry the bacon for 2 minutes. Remove it from the pan with a slotted spoon and reserve.

2. Lightly beat the eggs with the parsley and a pinch of salt and pepper. Pour the mixture into the frying pan and cook over a medium heat until it starts to set around the outside.

3. Use a spatula to draw the sides of the omelette into the centre, then tilt the pan to fill the gaps with more liquid egg. Repeat the process until the top of the omelette is almost set, then sprinkle over the bacon pieces.

4. Fold the omelette in half and serve immediately.

TOP TIP
Replace the bacon with thinly sliced mushrooms.

19

Smoked Salmon Scrambled Eggs

SERVES 1

PREPARATION TIME 10 MINUTES

COOKING TIME 4 MINUTES

INGREDIENTS

2 large eggs
25 g / 1 oz / ⅛ cup smoked salmon, chopped
2 tsp crème fraiche
1 chive, cut into short lengths
sea salt

METHOD

1. Break the eggs into a small saucepan, retaining the bigger half of the shells. Carefully rinse and dry the egg shells, then sit them inside two egg cups.

2. Gently beat the eggs in the saucepan with a pinch of salt.

3. Turn on the heat under the pan and stir the eggs until they scramble, then spoon them back into their shells.

4. Top each egg with smoked salmon and crème fraiche, then garnish with chives before serving.

TOP TIP
Top the finished eggs with a spoonful of caviar for an extra decadent treat.

Poached Egg and Salad on Toast

ERVES 4

REPARATION TIME 5 MINUTES

OOKING TIME 4 MINUTES

NGREDIENTS

tbsp white wine vinegar
large very fresh eggs
slices granary bread
tbsp butter
tomatoes, quartered
ixed salad leaves to serve
alt and black pepper

METHOD

1. Bring a wide saucepan of water to a gentle simmer and stir in the vinegar.

2. Crack each egg into a cup and pour them smoothly into the water, one at a time. Poach gently for 3 minutes.

3. Toast the bread lightly, then spread with the butter and top with the tomatoes and salad leaves.

4. Drain the eggs well, then sit them on top of the salad and sprinkle with salt and pepper.

TOP TIP

Top the egg with a Greek yogurt and a sprinkle of chilli (chili) flakes.

Fruity Rice Pudding

SERVES 6

PREPARATION TIME 15 MINUTES

COOKING TIME 10 MINUTES

INGREDIENTS

110 g / 4 oz / ½ cup short grain rice
75 g / 2 ½ oz / ¼ cup runny honey
1.2 litres / 2 pints / 4 ½ cups whole milk
4 tbsp sultanas
1 red apple, cored, quartered and very
    thinly sliced
3 tbsp crème fraiche
250 g / 9 oz / 1 ⅔ cups mixed summer berries
2 tbsp sunflower seeds

METHOD

1. Stir the rice, honey, milk, sultanas and apple together in a microwavable bowl, then cover with cling film and pierce the top.

2. Cook on high for 5 minutes, then stir well and cook for another 5 minutes or until all the milk has been absorbed and the rice is tender. Leave to stand for 5 minutes.

3. Divide the rice pudding between six bowls and spoon a little crème fraiche on top. Scatter over the berries and sprinkle with sunflower seeds before serving.

TOP TIP

This rice pudding also tastes great chilled if you make it in advance.

anana and azelnut ancakes

VES 4

PARATION TIME **5 MINUTES**

KING TIME **20 MINUTES**

REDIENTS

g / 9 oz / 1 ⅔ cups plain (all-purpose) flour

baking powder

ge eggs

ml / 10 ½ fl. oz / 1 ¼ cups milk

p butter

nanas, sliced

p Greek yogurt

p toasted hazelnuts (cobnuts), chopped

METHOD

1. Mix the flour and baking powder in a bowl and make a well in the centre. Break in the eggs and pour in the milk, then use a whisk to gradually incorporate all of the flour from round the outside.

2. Melt the butter in a small frying pan, then whisk it into the batter. Put the buttered frying pan back over a low heat. You will need 1 tbsp of batter for each pancake and you should be able to cook four pancakes at a time in the frying pan. Spoon the batter into the pan and drop a few slices of banana on top of each one.

3. Cook for 2 minutes or until small bubbles start to appear on the surface. Turn the pancakes over with a spatula and cook the other side until golden brown and cooked all the way through.

4. Repeat until all the batter has been used, keeping the finished batches warm in a low oven. Pile the pancakes onto warm plates and top each one with a spoonful of Greek yogurt, the rest of the sliced banana and a sprinkle of hazelnuts.

TOP TIP

Try replacing the hazelnuts with pecan nuts and add a drizzle of maple syrup.

Brown Sugar Porridge

SERVES **1**

PREPARATION TIME **5 MINUTES**

COOKING TIME **7 MINUTES**

INGREDIENTS

50 ml / 1 ¾ fl. oz / ¼ cup whole milk, plus extra
    to serve
40 g / 1 ½ oz / ½ cup oatmeal
1 tbsp brown sugar

METHOD

1. Bring the milk and 100 ml / 3 ½ fl. oz / ½
   of water to the boil, then stir in the oatm
   and a pinch of salt.

2. Simmer the porridge over a low heat for
   5–6 minutes, stirring occasionally. Add a
   little more water if it gets too thick.

3. Turn off the heat, cover the pan and leav
   the porridge to stand for 1 minute.

4. Spoon the porridge into a bowl and stir i
   the brown sugar. Top up with a little mor
   milk if you prefer a thinner consistency.

TOP TIP
Try topping the
porridge with a sliced
banana or a handful of
blueberries.

Melon with Prosciutto Grissini

SERVES **4**

PREPARATION TIME **25 MINUTES**

INGREDIENTS

small orange-fleshed melons
seedless watermelon
tbsp white port
thyme sprigs to garnish
grissini
slices prosciutto, halved

METHOD

1. Cut the tops off 4 of the melons in a zigzag pattern and scrape out the seeds with a spoon. Cut a small slice off the bases so that they stand upright without wobbling.

2. Cut the other melon in half and discard the seeds, then use a melon baller to scoop the flesh into spheres. Do the same with the watermelon, then pile the melon balls into the prepared melons. Spoon over the port and garnish with thyme.

3. Wrap the end of each grissini with half a slice of prosciutto and serve with the melons.

TOP TIP
You can also wrap the grissini with thinly sliced salami.

Coddled Eggs with Morcilla

SERVES **4**

PREPARATION TIME **10 MINUTES**

COOKING TIME **15 MINUTES**

INGREDIENTS

150 ml / 5 ½ fl. oz / ⅔ cup crème fraiche
4 large eggs
8 slices morcilla, or black pudding
½ tsp cumin seeds
2 slices bread
salt and black pepper

METHOD

1. Preheat the oven to 180°C (160°C fan) / 350F / gas 4.

2. Season the crème fraiche well with salt and pepper and divide it between four mini casserole dishes. Make a well in the centre and crack an egg into each one. Top with the morcilla slices and a sprinkle of the cumin seeds.

3. Sit the dishes in a roasting tin and pour enough boiling water around them to come halfway up the sides. Transfer the tin to the oven and bake for 15 minutes or until the whites of the eggs are set, but the yolks are still runny.

4. Toast the bread and cut it into soldiers, then serve with the coddled eggs.

TOP TIP
If you can't find morcilla, black pudding makes a good alternative.

Beef Carpaccio Crostini

METHOD

1. Slice the top and bottom off the orange. Slice away the peel, then cut out each individual segment, leaving the white pith behind. Discard the pith.

2. Toast the sourdough until crisp and golden brown, leave to cool for 2 minutes, then top with the salad leaves.

3. Massage the oil into the beef and season with a little salt, then arrange on top of the toast. Top with the orange segments and beetroot cubes and sprinkle with parsley and walnuts. Serve immediately.

KES 4

EPARATION TIME **15 MINUTES**

OKING TIME **2 MINUTES**

INGREDIENTS

ange
ices sourdough bread
andful of mixed salad leaves
sp extra virgin olive oil
afer-thin slices raw beef fillet
ooked beetroot, diced
sp flat leaf parsley, chopped
sp walnut pieces, chopped
salt

TOP TIP
Shave over a little Parmesan with a vegetable peeler for a tangy finish.

Preserved Vegetable and Prosciutto Crostini

MAKES 2

PREPARATION TIME 5 MINUTES

COOKING TIME 2 MINUTES

INGREDIENTS

2 slices sourdough bread
1 clove of garlic, halved
1 tbsp extra virgin olive oil
4 slices chargrilled aubergine (eggplant)
    in oil, drained
4 strips roasted red pepper in oil, drained
4 thin slices prosciutto
2 tsp thyme, chopped
black pepper

METHOD

1. Toast the sourdough until crisp and golden brown, then rub it vigorously all over with the cut side of a garlic clove. Drizzle the toast with oil.

2. Arrange the aubergine and pepper slices on top, then add the prosciutto and sprinkle with thyme and black pepper.

TOP TIP
Top the crostini with a few baby capers for a tangy finish.

Melon, Ham and Grape Salad

SERVES 4

PREPARATION TIME 4 MINUTES

INGREDIENTS

orange-fleshed melon
0 g / 5 ½ oz / 1 cup green seedless grapes, halved
0 g / 5 ½ oz / ⅔ cup honey roast ham, sliced
g / 1 ¾ oz / 2 cups lamb's lettuce
bsp white balsamic vinegar
lt and black pepper

METHOD

1. Use a melon baller to scoop the melon into spheres, then toss with the grapes, ham and lettuce.

2. Divide between four bowls and dress with the vinegar then season with salt and pepper.

TOP TIP

Top the salad with roasted, salted almonds for added crunch.

Pancakes with Raspberries and Honey

SERVES 2

PREPARATION TIME 5 MINUTES

COOKING TIME 25 MINUTES

INGREDIENTS

250 g / 9 oz / 1 ⅔ cups plain (all-purpose) flour
2 tsp baking powder
2 large eggs
300 ml / 10 ½ fl. oz / 1 ¼ cups milk
2 tbsp butter
4 tbsp runny honey
50 g / 1 ¾ oz / ⅔ cup raspberries

METHOD

1. Mix the flour and baking powder in a bowl and make a well in the centre. Break in the eggs and pour in the milk, then use a whisk to gradually incorporate all of the flour from round the outside.

2. Melt the butter in a frying pan, then whisk it into the batter. Put the buttered frying pan back over a low heat. You will need 1 tbsp of batter for each pancake and you should be able to cook four pancakes at a time in the frying pan.

3. Spoon the batter into the pan and cook for 2 minutes or until small bubbles start to appear on the surface. Turn the pancakes over with a spatula and cook the other side until golden brown and cooked through.

4. Repeat until all the batter has been used, keeping the finished batches warm in a low oven.

5. Pile the pancakes onto two warm plates and drizzle with the honey. Break the raspberries into small pieces with your fingers and scatter over the top.

TOP TIP
Add a few drops of rose water to the pancake batter for a floral aroma.

ggs Poached
n Tomato
auce

VES 2

PARATION TIME **2 MINUTES**

KING TIME **10 MINUTES**

REDIENTS

sp olive oil

ion, finely chopped

oves of garlic, crushed

ml / 10 ½ fl. oz / 1 ¼ cups tomato passata

rge eggs

sp Parmesan shavings

sp flat leaf parsley, shredded

and black pepper

METHOD

1. Heat the oil in a frying pan and fry the onion and garlic for 5 minutes without colouring. Stir in the passata and season with salt and pepper, then bring to a simmer.

2. Crack in the eggs, then reduce the heat. Put on the lid and poach gently for 4 minutes or until the whites are set, but the yolks are still a little runny.

3. Sprinkle with Parmesan and parsley and serve immediately.

TOP TIP

Top the finished dish with Greek yogurt and a sprinkle of chilli (chili) flakes.

Marinated Melon

SERVES 4

PREPARATION TIME 30 MINUTES

INGREDIENTS

1 white-fleshed melon
½ seedless watermelon
4 tbsp melon liqueur

METHOD

1. Cut the white-fleshed melon in half and scoop out the seeds. Cut into wedges, then cut away and discard the rind. Cut the flesh into bite-sized chunks.

2. Cut off the rind of the watermelon and discard, then cut the flesh into chunks and mix with the rest of the melon.

3. Spoon over the melon liqueur and leave to marinate for 15 minutes before serving.

TOP TIP

Sprinkle the melon with chopped pistachio nuts just before serving.

Lunches

Speedy Eggs Benedict

SERVES 2

PREPARATION TIME 15 MINUTES

COOKING TIME 4 MINUTES

INGREDIENTS

4 large eggs
2 bread rolls, halved
4 slices honey-roasted ham
1 tbsp lemon juice
1 tbsp French tarragon, chopped
3 tbsp mayonnaise
2 tbsp whipped cream

METHOD

1. Bring a large pan of water to a simmer. Oil a sheet of cling film and lay it, oil side up, in a mug. Break in an egg, then draw up the sides and twist them together to make a waterproof package. Repeat with three more pieces of cling film and the remaining eggs.

2. Lower the eggs into the simmering water and poach gently for 4 minutes.

3. Toast the rolls and lay a slice of ham on top of each half.

4. Stir the lemon juice and tarragon into the mayonnaise and fold in the whipped cream.

5. When the eggs are ready, remove and discard the cling film and lay them on top of the ham. Serve with the mayonnaise mixture on the side for spooning over at the table.

TOP TIP

Replace the ham with smoked salmon to make speedy eggs royale.

oats' Cheese
nd Prosciutto
agels

VES 2

PARATION TIME 5 MINUTES

KING TIME 2 MINUTES

REDIENTS

ces goats' cheese
thyme leaves
eded bagels, split in half
sp olive oil
ces prosciutto

METHOD

1. Preheat the grill to its highest setting.

2. Spread the goats' cheese slices out on a baking tray and sprinkle with thyme, then cook under the grill for 2 minutes or until the top of the cheese is lightly toasted.

3. Drizzle the bagel halves with oil, then arrange the prosciutto slices on top of the bottoms and position the toasted goats' cheese on top. Place the bagel tops on top and serve immediately.

TOP TIP
Try adding some sun-blushed tomatoes for a tangy flavour.

Scrambled Egg with Rocket

SERVES 4

PREPARATION TIME 2 MINUTES

COOKING TIME 5 MINUTES

INGREDIENTS

8 large eggs
2 tbsp butter
50 g / 1 ¾ oz / 1 cup rocket (arugula) leaves
4 English breakfast muffins, halved and toasted
salt and black pepper

METHOD

1. Gently beat the eggs with a pinch of salt and pepper to break up the yolks.

2. Heat the butter in a non-stick frying pan until sizzling, then pour in the eggs. Cook over a low heat, stirring constantly until the eggs scramble.

3. Stir in half of the rocket, then spoon it over the muffin halves.

4. Serve with extra rocket leaves on the side and a sprinkle of black pepper.

TOP TIP

Stir some cubed, pan-fried chorizo into the eggs when you add the rocket.

Chicken and Apple Salad

SERVES 2

PREPARATION TIME 5 MINUTES

COOKING TIME 6 MINUTES

INGREDIENTS

chicken breasts
Granny Smith apple, cored and quartered
lemon, halved
large carrot, grated
g / 2 ½ oz / ¾ cup cheese, cubed
tbsp sultanas
handful of lamb's lettuce
piece wholemeal toast
Salt and black pepper

METHOD

1. Preheat the grill to its highest setting.

2. Season the chicken with salt and pepper, then grill for 3 minutes on each side or until golden brown and cooked through.

3. Thinly slice the apple, then squeeze over the lemon juice to stop it from going brown.

4. Slice the chicken breasts and arrange them in two bowls with the apple, carrot, cheese, sultanas and lettuce. Tear the toast into rustic croutons and scatter over the top.

TOP TIP

Try topping the salad with a sprinkle of chopped walnuts for added crunch.

55

Monkfish and Sesame Seed Skewers

SERVES 2

PREPARATION TIME 20 MINUTES

COOKING TIME 6 MINUTES

INGREDIENTS

2 tbsp runny honey
1 tbsp lemon juice
1 tsp mild curry powder
225 g / 8 oz / 1 cup monkfish tail fillet, cubed
2 tbsp sesame seeds
1 tbsp flat leaf parsley, finely chopped
salt and black pepper

METHOD

1. Mix the honey, lemon juice and curry pow
   together and season with salt and pepper.
   Pour the mixture over the monkfish and
   leave to marinate for 15 minutes.

2. Meanwhile, soak six wooden skewers in
   a bowl of cold water.

3. Preheat the grill to its highest setting.
   Thread the monkfish onto the skewers and
   sprinkle with sesame seeds.

4. Cook the skewers under the grill for
   6 minutes, turning occasionally, or until
   the fish is only just cooked in the centre.
   Sprinkle with parsley and serve
   immediately.

TOP TIP

This recipe also works well with prawns or lobster.

Duck Skewers with Lemon Courgettes

METHOD

1. Stir the chilli jam and soy together, then massage it into the duck breasts. Leave to marinate for 10 minutes.

2. Preheat a griddle pan until smoking hot.

3. Thread the duck lengthways onto four skewers, then griddle for 3 minutes on each side or until nicely marked, but still pink in the centre.

4. Meanwhile, steam the courgette slices for 4 minutes. Squeeze the lemon over the courgette, then serve with the duck skewers.

SERVES 2

PREPARATION TIME **15 MINUTES**

COOKING TIME **6 MINUTES**

INGREDIENTS

tbsp chilli (chili) jam
tbsp dark soy sauce
duck breasts, skinned and halved lengthways
courgette (zucchini), cut into thick slices
lemon, halved

TOP TIP
This recipe also works well with lamb neck fillet.

Herb Omelette with Sun-blush Tomatoes

SERVES 1

PREPARATION TIME 5 MINUTES

COOKING TIME 6 MINUTES

INGREDIENTS

1 tbsp butter
2 large eggs
1 tbsp flat leaf parsley, finely chopped
1 tbsp chives, finely chopped
50 g / 1 ¾ oz / ½ cup sun-blush tomatoes in oil, drained and quartered
2 anchovy fillets, chopped
1 tsp capers, in brine, drained
salt and black pepper

METHOD

1. Heat the butter in a frying pan. Lightly beat the eggs with the herbs and a pinch of salt and pepper.

2. Pour the mixture into the frying pan and cook over a medium heat until it starts to set around the outside.

3. Use a spatula to draw the sides of the omelette into the centre, then tilt the pan to fill the gaps with more liquid egg.

4. Repeat the process until the top of the omelette is almost set, then turn it over and cook the other side.

5. Slide the omelette onto a chopping board and slice it into thick ribbons. Arrange the omelette with the tomatoes, anchovy and capers on a warm plate and serve immediately.

TOP TIP

Replace some of the sun-blush tomatoes with olives or artichokes.

oached Egg nd Bacon aps

RVES 4

PARATION TIME 2 MINUTES

KING TIME 5 MINUTES

GREDIENTS

ck rashers streaky bacon
ry fresh eggs
same baps
ctuce leaves
rge tomato, sliced
potatoes and salad to serve

METHOD

1. Preheat the grill to its highest setting and bring a wide saucepan of water to a gentle simmer.

2. Grill the bacon for 2 minutes on each side or until crisp and golden brown.

3. Meanwhile, crack each egg into a cup and pour them smoothly into the water, one at a time.

4. Simmer gently for 3 minutes. Slice the baps in half and add a lettuce leaf and a thick slice of tomato to the bottom halves.

5. Top the tomato with the bacon. Use a slotted spoon to take the eggs out of the water and blot the underneath on a piece of kitchen paper before laying them on top of the bacon.

6. Put the lids on the baps and hold everything together with a wooden skewer, then serve with new potatoes and salad.

TOP TIP

Replace the tomato slices with chargrilled red peppers in oil.

Chicken, Peach and Fennel Kebabs

SERVES 4

PREPARATION TIME 30 MINUTES

COOKING TIME 8 MINUTES

INGREDIENTS

½ tsp white peppercorns
½ tsp fennel seeds
½ tsp chilli flakes
1 clove garlic, crushed
3 tbsp olive oil
6 boneless skinless chicken thighs, cubed
2 small bulbs fennel, cut into chunks
3 peaches, cut into eighths

METHOD

1. Put 12 wooden skewers in a bowl of water and leave to soak for 20 minutes.

2. Meanwhile, grind the peppercorns, fennel seeds and chilli flakes together in a pestle and mortar, then add the garlic and oil and pound into a paste.

3. Scrape the paste into a large freezer bag, add the rest of the ingredients and massage together. Leave to marinate for 20 minutes.

4. Preheat the grill to its highest setting.

5. Thread alternate chunks of chicken, fennel and peach onto the skewers and spread them out on a large grill tray.

6. Grill the kebabs for 4 minutes on each side, or until they are golden brown and cooked through.

TOP TIP

Replace the peaches with apricots and the chicken with 450 g cubed lamb.

oconut Pancakes with weet and our Tuna

RVES **4**

EPARATION TIME **5 MINUTES**

OKING TIME **25 MINUTES**

GREDIENTS

g / 9 oz / 1 ⅔ cups plain (all-purpose) flour
p baking powder
rge eggs
ml / 10 ½ fl. oz / 1 ¼ cups coconut milk
sp butter
sp desiccated coconut

the tuna
g / 1 ¾ oz / ¼ cup brown sugar
ml / 1 ¾ fl. oz / ¼ cup rice wine vinegar
g / 5 ½ oz / ½ cup tomato ketchup
g / 5 ½ oz / 1 cup canned pineapple chunks
n juice
g / 5 ½ oz / 1 cup canned white tuna in
oil, drained
sp flat leaf parsley, chopped

METHOD

1. First prepare the tuna. Put all of the ingredients, except the tuna and parsley in a small saucepan and simmer for 5 minutes. Stir in the tuna and keep warm.

2. Meanwhile, mix the flour and baking powder in a bowl and make a well in the centre. Break in the eggs and pour in the coconut milk, then gradually incorporate all of the flour from round the outside using a whisk.

3. Melt the butter in a small frying pan, then whisk it into the batter with the desiccated coconut. Put the buttered frying pan back over a low heat. You will need 1 tbsp of batter for each pancake and you should be able to cook four pancakes at a time in the frying pan.

4. Spoon the batter into the pan and cook for 2 minutes or until small bubbles start to appear on the surface. Turn the pancakes over with a spatula and cook the other side until golden brown and cooked through.

5. Repeat until all the batter has been used, keeping the finished batches warm in a low oven. Serve the pancakes on warm plates with the tuna spooned over and sprinkle with parsley.

TOP TIP
Add a sprinkle of roughly chopped cashew nuts for added crunch.

Salad Tacos

METHOD

1. Lay the tortillas out on a chopping board and divide the lettuce between them.

2. Mix the tomato, onion, coriander and oil together and season with salt and pepper. Spoon the mixture on top of the lettuce.

3. Stir the lime juice into the soured cream, then drizzle it over the salsa, fold the tortillas in half and serve.

SERVES 4

PREPARATION TIME 5 MINUTES

INGREDIENTS

4 plain flour tortillas
¼ iceberg lettuce, shredded
4 tomatoes, diced
1 onion, finely chopped
3 tbsp coriander (cilantro) leaves, finely chopped
2 tbsp olive oil
1 tbsp lime juice
4 tbsp soured cream
salt and black pepper

TOP TIP

These tacos can be topped with pan-fried pieces of chicken, steak or chorizo.

Chickpea Pancakes with Tabbouleh

SERVES 4

PREPARATION TIME **10 MINUTES**

COOKING TIME **20 MINUTES**

INGREDIENTS

200 g / 9 oz / 1 ⅔ cups gram flour
1 tsp baking powder
2 large eggs
300 ml / 10 ½ fl. oz / 1 ¼ cups milk
1 tbsp butter

For the tabbouleh
150 g / 5 ½ oz / ¾ cup bulgar wheat
1 small bunch flat leaf parsley, finely chopped
2 tomatoes, deseeded and finely chopped
2 shallots, finely chopped
1 lemon, juiced
4 tbsp extra virgin olive oil
salt and black pepper

METHOD

1. Put the bulgar wheat in a bowl and pour over enough boiling water to just cover it. Cover the bowl with cling film and leave to soak for 15 minutes.

2. Meanwhile, mix the gram flour and baking powder in a bowl and make a well in the centre. Break in the eggs, then pour in the milk and use a whisk to gradually incorporate all of the flour from round the outside.

3. Melt the butter in a small frying pan, then whisk it into the batter. Put the buttered frying pan back over a low heat. You will need 1 tbsp of batter for each pancake and you should be able to cook four pancakes at a time in the frying pan.

4. Spoon the batter into the pan and cook for 2 minutes or until small bubbles start to appear on the surface. Turn the pancakes over with a spatula and cook the other side until golden brown and cooked through.

5. Repeat until all the batter has been used, keeping the finished batches warm in a low oven.

6. Tip the bulgar wheat into a sieve and run it under the cold tap to cool. Drain well. Stir the parsley, tomato and shallot into the bulgar and dress with the lemon juice and olive oil.

7. Season with salt and pepper, then serve with the pancakes.

TOP TIP

Spread the pancakes with hummus and top with spicy merguez sausage.

Brie and Tomato Toasts

SERVES 4

PREPARATION TIME **10 MINUTES**

COOKING TIME **10-12 MINUTES**

INGREDIENTS

4 slices sourdough bread
8 slices Brie
1 tomato, thinly sliced
1 tbsp fresh thyme leaves
a handful of rocket (arugula) leaves
olive oil, to drizzle

METHOD

1. Preheat the grill to its highest setting.

2. Toast the slices of sourdough on one side under the grill.

3. Turn them over and top each one with the Brie, tomatoes and a sprinkle of thyme.

4. Grill for 2 more minutes or until the cheese is bubbling and the bread is toasted at the edges.

5. Serve 2 toasts per plate with some rocket the side. Drizzle some olive oil over the rocket and sprinkle everything with fresh ground black pepper.

TOP TIP

Replace the tomatoes with a jar of roasted peppers in oil.

ardines Wrapped n Bacon

ES 2

ARATION TIME **10 MINUTES**

ING TIME **6 MINUTES**

REDIENTS

eless sardine fillets
igs rosemary
p pine nuts
hers unsmoked streaky bacon

METHOD

1. Preheat the grill to its highest setting.

2. Top each sardine fillet with a sprig of rosemary and 1 tbsp of pine nuts, then wrap tightly with bacon and secure with cocktail sticks.

3. Grill the sardine parcels for 3 minutes on each side or until the bacon is golden and crisp and the fish is just cooked in the centre. Serve immediately.

TOP TIP
This recipe also works really well with mackerel fillets.

Bacon, Potato and Spinach Frittata

SERVES 4

PREPARATION TIME **10 MINUTES**

COOKING TIME **12 MINUTES**

INGREDIENTS

150 g / 5 ½ oz / ¾ cup thin-cut smoked
    bacon, chopped
a large handful baby leaf spinach, chopped
75 g / 2 ½ oz / ½ cup boiled potatoes, cubed
6 large eggs, lightly beaten
1 tbsp butter
salt and black pepper

METHOD

1. Preheat the grill to its highest setting.

2. Stir the bacon, spinach and potatoes into the eggs and season with salt and pepper.

3. Melt the butter in an ovenproof frying pan, then pour in the egg mixture and cook on a gentle heat for 6–8 minutes or until the egg has set around the outside.

4. Put the frying pan under the grill to cook the top for 3–4 minutes or until golden brown and just set. Serve immediately.

TOP TIP

Try replacing the bacon with chorizo for a spicy kick.

weetcorn ancakes ith Roasted omatoes

ES **4**

ARATION TIME **5 MINUTES**

ING TIME **25 MINUTES**

REDIENTS

/ 9 oz / 1 ⅔ cups plain (all-purpose) flour
baking powder
ge eggs
nl / 10 ½ fl. oz / 1 ¼ cups milk
p butter
/ 7 oz / 1 cup canned sweetcorn, drained
ing onions (scallions), finely chopped
p olive oil
ato vines
leaves to serve
nd black pepper

METHOD

1. Preheat the oven to 190°C (170°C fan) / 375F / gas 5.

2. Mix the flour and baking powder in a bowl and make a well in the centre. Break in the eggs and pour in the milk, then use a whisk to gradually incorporate all of the flour from round the outside.

3. Melt the butter in a small frying pan, then whisk it into the batter with the sweetcorn and spring onions. Put the buttered frying pan back over a low heat. You will need 1 tbsp of batter for each pancake and you should be able to cook four pancakes at a time in the frying pan.

4. Spoon the batter into the pan and cook for 2 minutes or until small bubbles start to appear on the surface. Turn the pancakes over with a spatula and cook the other side until golden brown and cooked through.

5. Repeat until all the batter has been used, keeping the finished batches warm.

6. While the pancakes are cooking, drizzle the tomatoes with oil and roast on their vines for 10 minutes. Season with salt and pepper.

7. Serve the pancakes with the roast tomatoes and some fresh salad leaves.

TOP TIP

Serve with slices of pan-fried chorizo for a spicy kick.

Rigatoni with Broccoli and Lardons

SERVES **4**

PREPARATION TIME **5 MINUTES**

COOKING TIME **12 MINUTES**

INGREDIENTS

400 g / 14 oz / 3 ½ cups dried rigatoni
100 g / 3 ½ oz / 1 cup tenderstem broccoli
2 tbsp olive oil
100 g / 3 ½ oz / ½ cup lardons
1 lemon, zest finely pared
a handful of basil leaves
sea salt

METHOD

1. Cook the rigatoni in boiling, salted water according to the packet instructions or u 'al dente'. 4 minutes before the end of th cooking time, add the broccoli to the pan Drain well.

2. While the pasta is cooking, heat the oil in frying pan and fry the lardons for 4 minu or until golden brown.

3. Toss the pasta and broccoli with the lard then transfer to a warm serving dish and garnish with lemon zest and basil leaves

TOP TIP

This recipe tastes great with any pasta shapes – try penne or fusilli.

pinach nd Smoked almon rittata

RVES **4**

EPARATION TIME **5 MINUTES**

OKING TIME **12 MINUTES**

GREDIENTS

sp butter

rge eggs, lightly beaten

sp crème fraiche

g / 5 ½ oz / ¾ cup smoked salmon

rge handful baby leaf spinach

w chives, cut into short lengths

ck pepper

METHOD

1. Preheat the grill to its highest setting.

2. Melt the butter in an ovenproof frying pan. Pour in the eggs and cook over a gentle heat for 6–8 minutes or until the egg has set around the outside.

3. Put the frying pan under the grill to cook the top for 3–4 minutes or until golden brown and just set.

4. Spoon over the crème fraiche and arrange the smoked salmon on top. Scatter over the spinach and chives and serve immediately, sprinkled with black pepper.

TOP TIP

This recipe is delicious made with fresh crab meat in place of the smoked salmon.

Fusilli with Pesto and Tomatoes

SERVES 4

PREPARATION TIME 5 MINUTES

COOKING TIME 12 MINUTES

INGREDIENTS

400 g / 14 oz / 4 cups dried fusilli
100 g / 3 ½ oz / ½ cup pesto
100 g / 3 ½ oz / ⅔ cup cherry tomatoes,
    quartered
2 tbsp black olives, chopped
50 g / 1 ¾ oz / ½ cup piece of Parmesan
sea salt

METHOD

1. Cook the pasta in boiling, salted water according to the packet instructions or until 'al dente'.

2. Drain well, then stir in the pesto and toss with the cherry tomatoes and olives.

3. Divide the pasta between four warm bowls then use a vegetable peeler to shave some Parmesan over each one.

TOP TIP
Sprinkle the pasta with toasted pine nuts for added crunch.

rispy Chicken alad

VES 5

PARATION TIME **15 MINUTES**

KING TIME **4 MINUTES**

GREDIENTS

flower oil for deep-frying
/ 2 ½ oz / ½ cup dried breadcrumbs
sp basil leaves, finely chopped
sp Parmesan, finely grated
nless chicken breasts, cut into
ite-sized pieces
sp plain (all-purpose) flour
ge egg, beaten
g / 3 ½ oz / 2 cups baby leaf spinach
rd-boiled eggs, quartered
d pepper, quartered and thinly sliced
sp olive oil
sp lemon juice
runny honey
and black pepper

METHOD

1. Heat the sunflower oil in a deep fat fryer to 180°C, according to the manufacturer's instructions.

2. Mix the breadcrumbs with the basil and Parmesan and spread them out on a plate.

3. Dust the chicken breast pieces with flour, then dip them in egg and roll in the breadcrumb mixture to coat.

4. Fry the chicken pieces for 4 minutes or until golden brown and cooked through. Drain well on absorbent paper.

5. Arrange the spinach leaves on four plates and top with the chicken, egg and sliced pepper. Whisk together the olive oil, lemon juice and honey and season to taste, then drizzle it over the salad.

TOP TIP

Use chicken thigh instead of chicken breast for an extra juicy texture.

Club Sandwich

SERVES **1**

PREPARATION TIME **5 MINUTES**

COOKING TIME **4 MINUTES**

INGREDIENTS

3 slices white bread, crusts removed
4 rashers smoked streaky bacon
4 slices cheese
½ cooked chicken breast, sliced
a handful of rocket (arugula)

METHOD

1. Preheat the grill to its highest setting.
   Grill the bread and bacon for 2 minutes,
   then turn everything over and top two
   of the bread slices with cheese. Grill for
   2 more minutes or until the bacon is
   crisp and the cheese has melted.

2. Top the cheese toasts with bacon,
   chicken and rocket.

3. Press the plain slices of toast firmly on
   top of the cheese and bacon toasts, then
   cut in half diagonally and secure each
   half together with a cocktail stick.

TOP TIP

Add a sliced avocado to the sandwich for a buttery-smooth texture.

horizo, Mozzarella and Sun-dried Tomato Rolls

METHOD

1. Preheat the oven to 180°C (160°C fan) / 350F / gas 4.

2. Cut the rolls in half lengthways and spread one side of each one with pesto.

3. Drain the sun-dried tomatoes and layer them up in the rolls with the mozzarella and chorizo.

4. Wrap each baton in foil and bake for 10 minutes to melt the cheese, then serve warm.

RVES **4**

EPARATION TIME **5 MINUTES**

OKING TIME **10 MINUTES**

GREDIENTS

heese baton rolls
osp pesto
g / 1 ¾ oz / ¼ cup sun-dried tomatoes
in oil, drained
alls light mozzarella, cubed
g / 1 ¾ oz / ¼ cup chorizo, thinly sliced

TOP TIP

For a vegetarian alternative, replace the chorizo with pitted green olives.

91

Cheese and Sun-dried Tomato Rice Salad

SERVES 4

PREPARATION TIME 10 MINUTES

COOKING TIME 20 MINUTES

INGREDIENTS

200 g / 7 oz / 1 cup long grain rice
1 tbsp runny honey
½ lemon, juiced
150 g / 5 ½ oz / ¾ cup reduced-fat hard
    cheese, cubed
100 g / 3 ½ oz / ¾ cup sun-dried tomatoes in oil,
    drained and chopped
2 tbsp chives, chopped
salt and black pepper

METHOD

1. Put the rice in a saucepan and add enoug
   water to cover it by 1 cm (½ in).

2. Bring the pan to the boil, then cover and
   turn down the heat to its lowest setting.

3. Cook for 10 minutes, then turn off the hea
   and leave to stand, without lifting the lid,
   for 10 minutes.

4. Whisk the honey with the lemon juice
   to make a dressing and season with salt
   and pepper.

5. When the rice is ready, stir in the dressing
   cheese and tomatoes and garnish with
   chopped chives.

TOP TIP
Stir through a handful of toasted pine nuts for added crunch.

Melon
Gazpacho

METHOD

1. Scoop the flesh out of the melon into a liquidizer and add the cucumber, vinegar and oil.

2. Blend until smooth, then pass the mixture through a sieve and season to taste with salt and pepper.

3. Pour into four bowls and garnish with mint leaves.

SERVES 4

PREPARATION TIME 10 MINUTES

INGREDIENTS

large orange-fleshed melon, halved
and deseeded
cucumber, peeled and diced
sherry vinegar
extra virgin olive oil
leaves to garnish
and black pepper

TOP TIP

Try topping the gazpacho with crumbled feta for a tangy finish.

Tomatoes Stuffed with Goats' Cheese

SERVES 2

PREPARATION TIME 20 MINUTES

COOKING TIME 30 SECONDS

INGREDIENTS

6 medium tomatoes
400 g / 14 oz / 1 ¾ cups soft goats' cheese
1 lemon, zest finely grated
2 tbsp flat leaf parsley, finely chopped
2 tbsp chives, finely chopped
2 tbsp basil leaves, finely chopped
extra herbs to garnish
salt and black pepper

METHOD

1. Score a cross in the top of each tomato, then blanch them in boiling water for 30 seconds. Plunge into iced water, then peel off the skins.

2. Cut a small slice from one side of each tomato. Use a melon baller to remove the core and seeds of the tomatoes.

3. Mix the goats' cheese with the lemon zest and herbs and season to taste with salt and pepper.

4. Pack the goats' cheese mixture into the tomatoes, then serve immediately, garnished with extra herbs.

TOP TIP
Try using the goats' cheese mixture to stuff fresh figs when they're in season.

ream of
ushroom
oup

ES 4

ARATION TIME **5 MINUTES**

ING TIME **25 MINUTES**

REDIENTS

olive oil
butter
n, finely chopped
es of garlic, crushed
/ 14 oz / 5 ⅓ cups flat cap mushrooms,
opped
/ 1 pint 15 fl. oz / 4 cups vegetable stock
l / 3 ½ fl. oz / ½ cup double (heavy) cream,
us extra to garnish
of grated nutmeg
ed flat leaf parsley to garnish
nd black pepper

METHOD

1. Heat the oil and butter in a saucepan and fry the onion for 5 minutes or until softened.

2. Add the garlic and mushrooms to the pan and cook for 5 more minutes, then stir in the vegetable stock and bring to the boil.

3. Simmer for 15 minutes, then stir in the double cream and nutmeg.

4. Blend the soup with a liquidizer or stick blender until smooth, then season to taste with salt and pepper.

5. Ladle into warm mugs, then add a swirl of cream and a sprinkle of parsley to each one.

TOP TIP
Add 2 tbsp of chopped thyme leaves when you cook the garlic.

Lentil and Sweet Potato Soup

SERVES 4

PREPARATION TIME 5 MINUTES

COOKING TIME 25 MINUTES

INGREDIENTS

400 g / 14 oz / 3 ¼ cups red lentils
1 small sweet potato, peeled and diced
2 cloves of garlic, crushed
1 tbsp fresh root ginger, finely chopped
2 tsp mild curry powder
1.2 litres / 2 pints / 5 cups vegetable stock
2 tbsp crème fraiche
coriander (cilantro) to garnish
salt and black pepper

METHOD

1. Put the lentils, sweet potato, garlic, ginger, curry powder and vegetable stock in a saucepan and bring to the boil. Turn down the heat and simmer for 25 minutes or until the lentils and potato are completely tender.

2. Transfer the soup to a liquidizer and blend until smooth. Season to taste with salt and pepper.

3. Ladle the soup into warm bowls and top with a spoonful of crème fraiche and a sprinkle of coriander.

TOP TIP
The sweet potatoes can be replaced with butternut squash.

Orzo Pasta with Rocket and Parmesan

METHOD

1. Cook the orzo in a large pan of boiling salted water according to the packet instructions or until 'al dente'.

2. Drain well, then stir in the rocket and pesto. Season to taste with salt and pepper.

3. Divide the pasta between two bowls and scatter over the Parmesan shavings.

SERVES 2

PREPARATION TIME 5 MINUTES

COOKING TIME 10 MINUTES

INGREDIENTS

200 g / 7 oz / 1 cup dried orzo pasta
50 g / 1 ¾ oz / 1 cup rocket (arugula), chopped
2 tbsp pesto
2 tbsp Parmesan shavings
Sea salt and black pepper

TOP TIP
For a gluten-free alternative, use basmati rice instead of the orzo pasta.

Scallop Gratin

SERVES 4

PREPARATION TIME 15 MINUTES

COOKING TIME 15 MINUTES

INGREDIENTS

12 scallops in the half shell, cleaned
2 tbsp butter
1 shallot, finely chopped
1 clove of garlic, crushed
1 tbsp plain (all-purpose) flour
150 ml / 5 ½ fl. oz / ⅔ cup dry white wine
300 ml / 10 ½ fl. oz / 1 ¼ cups whole milk
a little freshly grated nutmeg
2 tbsp dried breadcrumbs
3 tbsp Gruyère cheese, grated
salt and black pepper

METHOD

1. Preheat the oven to 190°C (170°C fan) / 375F / gas 5.

2. Carefully slice the scallops away from the shells and reserve four shells. Discard the rest. Arrange 3 scallops in the shells and s them in a roasting tin.

3. Heat the butter in a saucepan and fry the shallot and garlic for 2 minutes to soften without colouring. Stir in the flour, then whisk in the wine, followed by the milk. Whisk gently until the mixture starts to bubble and thicken. Cook out the flour for 2 minutes, then season to taste with salt, pepper and nutmeg.

4. Spoon the sauce on top of the scallops. Mix the breadcrumbs with the cheese and sprinkle it over the top, then bake the scallops for 15 minutes or until golden brown and bubbling. Serve immediately.

TOP TIP
This recipe also works really well with oysters in place of the scallops.

oasted Fig nd Goats' heese Salad

VES 2

PARATION TIME **5 MINUTES**

KING TIME **5 MINUTES**

REDIENTS

e figs, quartered
sp runny honey
g / 3 ½ oz / ½ cup crumbled goats' cheese
/ 1 ¾ oz / 1 cup baby spinach leaves
ces prosciutto, thinly shredded
sp basil leaves
p smoked paprika
and pepper

METHOD

1. Preheat the oven to 180°C (160°C fan) / 350F / gas 4.

2. Spread the figs out in a roasting tin and drizzle with honey. Season with salt and pepper then roast for 5 minutes.

3. Toss the warm figs with the goats' cheese and spinach leaves, then divide between two bowls.

4. Scatter over the shredded ham and basil leaves and sprinkle with paprika, then serve immediately.

TOP TIP

Try replacing the goats' cheese with feta.

Main Meals

Grilled Tuna Steak with Peppers

SERVES 2

PREPARATION TIME 5 MINUTES

COOKING TIME 12 MINUTES

INGREDIENTS

2 tbsp olive oil
1 red pepper, deseeded and diced
1 yellow pepper, deseeded and diced
1 green pepper, deseeded and diced
1 clove of garlic, finely chopped
1 tbsp runny honey
2 tbsp sherry vinegar
2 tuna steaks
salt and black pepper

METHOD

1. Preheat the grill to its highest setting.

2. Heat the oil in a frying pan, then fry the peppers for 8 minutes or until starting to soften. Add the garlic to the pan and fry for 1 more minute, then stir in the honey and vinegar and season with salt and pepper. Cook for 2 more minutes.

3. Meanwhile, season the tuna steaks with salt and pepper, then grill for 2 minutes on each side or until cooked to your liking.

4. Serve the steaks with the peppers on the side.

TOP TIP

Try replacing the tuna steaks with swordfish steaks.

od with
atay Sauce

METHOD

1. Preheat the oven to 190°C (170°C fan) / 375F / gas 5 and put the cod in a baking dish.

2. Mix together the peanut butter, honey, soy sauce, lime juice and 5-spice, then pour it over the cod.

3. Bake the cod for 15 minutes or until just cooked in the centre, then serve with the rice and the sauce from the dish spooned over.

'ES 4

'ARATION TIME 5 MINUTES

ING TIME 15 MINUTES

REDIENTS

tions cod fillet
crunchy peanut butter
runny honey
light soy sauce
e, juiced
Chinese 5-spice powder
d rice to serve

TOP TIP

The cod can be replaced with any white fish, try pollock or coley.

Mustard Pork Chops with Quick Peach Chutney

METHOD

1. Preheat the grill to its highest setting.

2. Spread the pork chops with mustard, th grill for 3 minutes on each side or until j cooked in the centre.

3. Meanwhile, heat the oil in a saucepan ar fry the onion, ginger and chilli for 5 min Stir in the peaches, pepper, honey and vinegar then simmer for 5 minutes.

4. Serve the chops with the warm chutney on the side and garnish with coriander.

SERVES 4

PREPARATION TIME 8 MINUTES

COOKING TIME 12 MINUTES

INGREDIENTS

4 small pork chops
4 tbsp grain mustard
2 tbsp olive oil
1 onion, finely chopped
1 tsp fresh root ginger, finely chopped
1 red chilli (chili), finely chopped
2 peaches, peeled, stoned and diced
100 g / 3 ½ oz / ½ cup roasted red peppers in oil,
    drained and chopped
2 tbsp runny honey
2 tbsp rice wine vinegar
coriander (cilantro) to garnish

TOP TIP

The chutney makes a great condiment for duck breast too.

uote with omatoes and rosciutto

VES **4**

PARATION TIME **5 MINUTES**

KING TIME **12 MINUTES**

REDIENTS

g / 3 ½ oz / ²/₃ cup cherry tomatoes
g / 14 oz / 4 cups dried ruote pasta
g / 3 ½ oz / ²/₃ cup frozen peas, defrosted
ces prosciutto, chopped
sp Parmesan, grated
ndful of mint leaves
sp extra virgin olive oil
and black pepper

METHOD

1. Preheat the oven to 190°C (170°C fan) / 375F / gas 5. Roast the tomatoes whole for 10 minutes.

2. Cook the pasta in boiling, salted water according to the packet instructions or until 'al dente'. 2 minutes before the end of the cooking time, add the peas. Drain well, then toss with the roasted tomatoes and prosciutto.

3. Divide between four warm bowls and top with the Parmesan and mint, then dress with olive oil, salt and pepper.

TOP TIP
You can also make this recipe with smoked salmon in place of the prosciutto.

Steak and Potato Wedges

SERVES 2

PREPARATION TIME 8 MINUTES

COOKING TIME 15 MINUTES

INGREDIENTS

sunflower oil for deep-frying
4 medium potatoes, cut into wedges
2 T-bone steaks
2 tbsp butter, softened
1 clove of garlic, crushed
1 tbsp flat leaf parsley; finely chopped
salad leaves to serve
salt and black pepper

METHOD

1. Preheat the grill to its highest setting and heat the oil in a deep fat fryer, according the manufacturer's instructions, to a temperature of 130°C.

2. Lower the wedges in the fryer basket and cook for 10 minutes so that they cook all way through but don't brown.

3. Pull up the fryer basket and increase the fryer temperature to 190°C. When the oil has come up to temperature, lower the f basket and cook the wedges for 5 minute or until crisp and golden brown.

4. While the wedges are cooking, season th steaks with salt and pepper and grill for 4 minutes on each side or until cooked to your liking. Leave to rest somewhere wa while you finish the wedges.

5. Mix the butter with the garlic and parsley then shape into two butter pats.

6. Top each steak with a garlic butter pat ar serve with the wedges and salad leaves.

TOP TIP
Try mashing a handful of blue cheese into the butter.

paghetti alla arbonara

VES **2**

PARATION TIME **5 MINUTES**

KING TIME **12 MINUTES**

REDIENTS

g / 7 oz / 2 cups dried spaghetti
ck rashers pancetta, diced
sp olive oil
ve of garlic, crushed
ge egg
/ 1 ¾ oz / ½ cup Parmesan, finely grated
and black pepper

METHOD

1. Bring a large pan of salted water to the boil and cook the spaghetti according to the packet instructions or until 'al dente'.

2. Meanwhile, fry the pancetta in the oil for 4 minutes or until golden brown. Add the garlic and cook for 2 more minutes, then turn off the heat.

3. Beat the egg and stir in half the grated Parmesan with plenty of black pepper.

4. When the spaghetti is ready, reserve a ladleful of the cooking water and drain the rest.

5. Tip the spaghetti into the bacon pan and pour in the egg mixture. Mix it all together, adding enough of the cooking water to make a thick shiny sauce that clings to the pasta.

6. Divide between two warm bowls and sprinkle over the rest of the Parmesan and some more black pepper.

TOP TIP

Stir a big handful of chopped parsley through the pasta.

Lemon and Herb Pork Steaks

SERVES 4

PREPARATION TIME 2 MINUTES

COOKING TIME 10 MINUTES

INGREDIENTS

4 thick pork steaks
2 tbsp olive oil
a small knob of butter
1 tsp rosemary, chopped
4 sprigs oregano, chopped
1 lemon, halved
salad leaves to serve
salt and black pepper

METHOD

1. Season the steaks liberally with salt and pepper.

2. Heat the oil in a large frying pan, then add the steaks and cook for 3 minutes.

3. Turn them over and cook for 3 minutes or until just cooked in the centre.

4. Transfer the steaks to four warm plates. Add the butter and herbs to the pan and swirl until the butter melts.

5. Squeeze in the lemon juice, then spoon the pan juices over the steaks and serve immediately with salad leaves.

TOP TIP
Try replacing the lemon with orange for a sweeter flavour.

esto-stuffed ork

ES 4

ARATION TIME **15 MINUTES**

ING TIME **8 MINUTES**

REDIENTS

k pork steaks
 pesto
 pine nuts, roughly chopped
 1 oz / ¼ cup Parmesan shavings
es prosciutto, chopped
n dauphinoise to serve

METHOD

1. Preheat the grill to its highest setting.

2. Cut a deep pocket into the side of each pork steak with a sharp knife. Mix the pesto with the pine nuts and Parmesan and stuff the mixture into the pockets.

3. Grill the pork steaks for 4 minutes on each side or until golden brown and cooked through.

4. Transfer the steaks to 4 warm plates and sprinkle over the prosciutto, then serve with gratin dauphinoise.

TOP TIP
Try using this stuffing with chicken too.

Tagliatelle with Prosciutto and Tomatoes

SERVES **4**

PREPARATION TIME **5 MINUTES**

COOKING TIME **12 MINUTES**

INGREDIENTS

400 g / 14 oz / 4 cups dried tagliatelle
6 slices prosciutto, chopped
100 g / 3 ½ oz / ⅔ cup cherry tomatoes,
    quartered
a handful of rocket (arugula)
a handful of basil leaves
4 tbsp extra virgin olive oil
sea salt and black pepper

METHOD

1. Cook the tagliatelle in boiling, salted w
according to the packet instructions or
'al dente'. Drain well.

2. Return the pasta to the saucepan and to
with the rest of the ingredients, then di
between four warm plates and serve
immediately.

TOP TIP

Top the pasta with a
little freshly grated
lemon zest for
extra zing.

Salmon with chorizo and aubergine

SERVES 4

PREPARATION TIME 10 MINUTES

COOKING TIME 15 MINUTES

INGREDIENTS

portions of salmon fillet

g / 8 oz / 1 ½ cups chorizo ring, sliced

small aubergines (eggplants), sliced lengthways

tbsp olive oil

lemon, juiced

tbsp flat leaf parsley, chopped

tsp smoked paprika

METHOD

1. Preheat the oven to 190°C (170°C fan) / 375F / gas 5.

2. Spread out the salmon portions in a single layer in a roasting tin and arrange the chorizo slices on top to look like scales. Bake the salmon for 15 minutes, until the fish has just turned opaque in the centre.

3. Meanwhile, brush the aubergine slices with half of the oil. Griddle for 5 minutes on each side or until softened and nicely marked. Transfer to a shallow bowl.

4. Mix the rest of the oil with the lemon juice and parsley and drizzle it over the aubergine.

5. Divide the salmon between four warm plates and sprinkle with paprika.

6. Spoon the aubergine slices alongside the salmon with their dressing and serve immediately.

TOP TIP

This recipe also works really well with cod in place of the salmon.

Bunless Egg and Onion Burgers

SERVES 2

PREPARATION TIME 10 MINUTES

COOKING TIME 16 MINUTES

INGREDIENTS

450 g / 1 lb / 2 cups beef mince
2 tbsp double (heavy) cream
1 tsp Dijon mustard
4 tbsp sunflower oil
1 large onion, sliced into rings
4 large eggs
½ tsp paprika
mixed salad leaves and barbecue sauce, to serve
salt and black pepper

METHOD

1. Mix the beef with the cream and mustard and season generously, then knead light until sticky. Divide the mixture into four and press each piece into a ring mould to get an even shape.

2. Heat half of the oil in a frying pan, then fr the burgers for 8 minutes, turning every 2 minutes. Wrap the burgers in a double layer of foil and leave them to rest while you cook the eggs and onions.

3. Add another tablespoon of oil to the pan and fry the onion rings for 2 minutes on each side or until they're just starting to brown and soften.

4. Add the final tablespoon of oil to the pan and put the burger ring moulds in to heat Crack and egg into each one and sprinkle the tops with paprika. Cook for 4 minutes or until the whites are set, but the yolks are still a little runny.

5. Top the burgers with the onion and eggs and serve with the salad leaves and barbecue sauce on the side.

TOP TIP

Add a few slices of crispy bacon for extra decadence.

Macaroni with Courgette and Smoked Salmon

SERVES 4

PREPARATION TIME 5 MINUTES

COOKING TIME 20 MINUTES

INGREDIENTS

g / 14 oz / 3 cups dried elbow macaroni
urgettes (zucchinis), halved and thinly sliced
Dijon mustard
sp crème fraiche
ces smoked salmon, chopped
/ 1 ¾ oz / ½ cup Emmental, grated
salt

METHOD

1. Preheat the oven to 190°C (170°C fan) / 375F / gas 5.

2. Cook the macaroni in boiling, salted water for 5 minutes. Add the courgettes and cook for 3 more minutes or until the macaroni is 'al dente'. Drain well.

3. Stir the mustard into the crème fraiche, then stir it into the macaroni and courgettes with the smoked salmon.

4. Spoon the pasta mixture into a greased baking dish and sprinkle the top with cheese. Bake the macaroni for 10 minutes or until the top is golden brown.

TOP TIP
Try prosciutto instead of the smoked salmon.

Swordfish with Tomato and Passion Fruit Salsa

SERVES **2**

PREPARATION TIME **10 MINUTES**

COOKING TIME **4 MINUTES**

INGREDIENTS

2 swordfish steaks
1 small onion, finely chopped
4 medium tomatoes, deseeded and finely diced
½ clove of garlic, crushed
2 tbsp coriander (cilantro) leaves, finely chopped
2 passion fruit, halved
salt and black pepper

METHOD

1. Preheat the grill to its highest setting.

2. Season the swordfish with salt, then grill for 2 minutes on each side or until cooked to your liking.

3. Meanwhile, stir the onion, tomato, garlic and coriander together. Pass the passion fruit pulp through a sieve to remove the seeds, then stir the juice into salsa. Season to taste with salt and pepper.

4. Spoon the salsa over the swordfish and serve immediately.

TOP TIP

Try replacing the tomatoes with mango for a tropical taste.

Pepperoni and Green Pepper Pizza

SERVES 2

PREPARATION TIME **2 MINUTES**

COOKING TIME **12 MINUTES**

INGREDIENTS

Large pizza base
4 tbsp passata sauce
100 g / 3 ½ oz / 1 cup mozzarella, sliced
100 g / 3 ½ oz / 1 cup pepperoni, sliced
1 green pepper, sliced
Few sprigs mint

METHOD

1. Preheat the oven to 220°C (200°C fan) / 430 F / gas 7 and put a baking tray in to heat.

2. Spread the pizza base thinly with passata and arrange the mozzarella slices on top.

3. Scatter over the pepperoni and green pepper and sprinkle with black pepper.

4. Bake the pizza for 10 minutes or until the toppings are bubbling.

5. Garnish with mint and serve immediately.

TOP TIP

For a spicy kick, mix ½ tsp chilli (chili) flakes into the passata first.

Grilled Prawns with Stir-fried Noodles

SERVES 4

PREPARATION TIME 5 MINUTES

COOKING TIME 10 MINUTES

INGREDIENTS

200 g / 7 oz / 2 cups thin egg noodles
16 raw king prawns (shrimp)
3 tbsp vegetable oil
2 cloves of garlic, julienned
1 tbsp root ginger, julienned
1 carrot, julienned
50 g / 1 ¾ oz / ½ cup green beans, thinly sliced
    lengthways
¼ pineapple, peeled, cored and thinly sliced
2 tbsp light soy sauce
50 g / 1 ¾ oz / ½ cup bean sprouts
a few sprigs coriander (cilantro)

METHOD

1. Cook the noodles in boiling salted water according to the packet instructions or until al dente, then drain well.

2. Preheat the grill to its highest setting.

3. Spread the prawns out on a large grill tray and grill for 2 minutes on each side or until opaque.

4. Meanwhile, heat the oil in a large wok and fry the garlic and ginger for 30 seconds.

5. Add the carrot, beans and pineapple and stir-fry for 2 minutes then add the soy, beansprouts and noodles and cook for 2 minutes.

6. Serve the noodles in warm bowls, garnished with coriander, with the prawns on the side.

TOP TIP

Thin strips of chicken, beef or pork can be used to replace the prawns.

Rib-eye with Tomatoes

SERVES 1

PREPARATION TIME 10 MINUTES

COOKING TIME 6 MINUTES

INGREDIENTS

large rib-eye steak
tbsp olive oil
sprig of rosemary
clove of garlic, halved
cherry tomatoes, halved
salt and black pepper

METHOD

1. Put a frying pan over a high heat and season the steak liberally with salt and pepper.

2. Drizzle the oil over the base of the pan then lower in the steak and add the rosemary, garlic and tomatoes, cut side down, next to it.

3. Cook without disturbing for 3 minutes, then turn everything over and cook for another 3 minutes. If you prefer your steak well-done, cook it for another 2–3 minutes on each side.

4. Wrap the steak in a double layer of foil and leave to rest for 5 minutes, then serve with the tomatoes.

TOP TIP
Try replacing the tomatoes with baby button mushrooms.

Rigatoni with Tomatoes and Feta

SERVES **2**

PREPARATION TIME **5 MINUTES**

COOKING TIME **12 MINUTES**

INGREDIENTS

200 g / 7 oz / 2 cups dried rigatoni
100 g / 3 ½ oz / ⅔ cup feta, crumbled
100 g / 3 ½ oz / ⅔ cup cherry tomatoes, halved
4 slices cooked ham, chopped
a handful of basil leaves
4 tbsp olive oil
2 tbsp Parmesan, finely grated
salt and black pepper

METHOD

1. Cook the rigatoni in boiling, salted water according to the packet instructions or until 'al dente'.

2. Drain well, then toss with the feta, tomatoes, ham and basil leaves.

3. Divide between two warm bowls and dress with the olive oil, then sprinkle with Parmesan and black pepper.

TOP TIP
Try replacing the feta with crumbled Stilton.

Mushroom Fricassée with Eggs

ES 2

PARATION TIME **10 MINUTES**

KING TIME **20 MINUTES**

REDIENTS

p olive oil
p butter
/ 5 ½ oz / 2 cups button mushrooms, halved
hers streaky bacon, halved
ve of garlic, crushed
l / 1 ¾ oz / ¼ cup dry white wine
nl / 3 ½ fl. oz / ½ cup double (heavy) cream,
us extra to garnish
ge eggs
p Parmesan, finely grated
eaf parsley to garnish

METHOD

1. Preheat the oven to 180°C (160°C fan) / 350F / gas 4.

2. Heat the oil and butter in a sauté pan and fry the mushrooms and bacon for 5 minutes, stirring occasionally. Stir in the garlic and cook for 1 more minute, then pour in the wine and reduce by half. Stir in the cream and simmer for 2 minutes.

3. Scrape the mixture into an enamel baking dish and break in the eggs. Transfer the dish to the oven and bake for 10 minutes or until the egg whites are just set.

4. Sprinkle over the Parmesan and garnish with parsley then serve immediately.

TOP TIP

Try replacing the bacon with chorizo for a spicy kick.

Artichoke and Feta Pasta Salad

SERVES **4**

PREPARATION TIME **10 MINUTES**

COOKING TIME **12 MINUTES**

INGREDIENTS

300 g / 11 oz / 3 cups dried rigatoni
100 g / 3 ½ oz / 3 cups baby leaf spinach
300 g / 10 ½ oz / 1 ½ cups artichokes in oil,
   drained and quartered
75 g / 2 ½ oz / ½ cup black olives
100 g / 3 ½ oz / ⅔ cup feta, crumbled
150 g / 5 ½ oz / 1 cup cherry tomatoes, halved
4 tbsp olive oil
1 lemon, juiced
½ clove of garlic, crushed
½ tsp dried chilli (chili) flakes
salt and black pepper

METHOD

1. Cook the rigatoni in boiling, salted water according to the packet instructions or until 'al dente'. Drain well, then plunge into iced water to quickly cool it to room temperature. Drain again.

2. Toss the pasta with the spinach, artichokes, olives, feta and cherry tomatoes.

3. Whisk the oil with the lemon juice, garlic and chilli flakes and season generously with salt and pepper. Toss the dressing with the salad, then divide between four bowls and serve immediately.

TOP TIP
Try replacing the olives with capers.

146

Lamb Chops with Cheese, Tomato and Bacon

METHOD

1. Preheat the oven to 200°C (180°C fan) / 400F / gas 6.

2. Top each lamb chop with a slice of Brie and a slice of tomato, then wrap them tightly in the bacon. Transfer the chops to a roasting tin and surround with the lemon wedges, then roast for 20 minutes.

3. Serve the chops with the roasted lemon wedges for squeezing over.

SERVES 2

PREPARATION TIME 5 MINUTES

COOKING TIME 20 MINUTES

INGREDIENTS

lamb chops, French trimmed
slices Brie
tomato, sliced
rashers streaky bacon
lemon, cut into wedges

TOP TIP

This recipe also works really well with pork chops.

Blackened Duck Breast with Cherry Tomatoes

SERVES 2

PREPARATION TIME 20 MINUTES

COOKING TIME 10 MINUTES

INGREDIENTS

2 tbsp runny honey
1 tsp Dijon mustard
½ tbsp Worcestershire sauce
½ tsp dried rosemary
2 duck breasts
200 g / 7 oz / 1 ⅓ cups cherry tomatoes on
    the vine

METHOD

1. Preheat the oven to 220°C (200°C fan)
   / 425F / gas 7.

2. Mix the honey, mustard, Worcestershire
   sauce and rosemary together and massage
   it into the duck breasts. Leave to marinate
   for 10 minutes.

3. Transfer the duck breasts to a roasting tin
   and lay the tomato vines next to them, then
   roast for 10 minutes or until the duck is
   deeply caramelized on the outside, but
   still pink in the middle.

4. Leave the duck to rest for 5 minutes,
   then slice and serve with the tomatoes.

TOP TIP

For extra depth of flavour, marinade the duck for up to 4 hours before cooking.

Stuffed Chicken Breast with Root Vegetables

RVES **4**

EPARATION TIME **2 MINUTES**

OKING TIME **30 MINUTES**

GREDIENTS

arrots, quartered
arsnips, cut into thin wedges
osp olive oil
osp butter
hallot, finely chopped
arlic clove, crushed
g / 1 oz / ⅓ cup fresh breadcrumbs
g / 1 ¾ oz / ⅓ cup pine nuts, finely chopped
osp basil leaves, finely chopped
osp Parmesan, finely grated
hicken breasts, skin-on
t and black pepper

METHOD

1. Preheat the oven to 220°C (200°C fan) / 430F / gas 7. Put the carrots and parsnips in a roasting tin and drizzle with olive oil, then roast in the oven for 10 minutes.

2. Meanwhile, heat the butter in a frying pan and fry the shallot and garlic for 4 minutes or until softened but not coloured. Take the pan off the heat and stir in the breadcrumbs, pine nuts, basil and Parmesan, then season with salt and pepper.

3. Cut a deep pocket into the side of the chicken breasts and fill with the stuffing mixture.

4. Transfer the chicken to the roasting tin, reduce the temperature to 190°C (170°C fan) / 375F / gas 5 and cook for 18 minutes until the chicken is cooked through and the vegetables are tender.

5. Serve the chicken immediately with the root vegetables on the side.

TOP TIP

Use chicken thigh quarters instead of the breasts. Make a pocket in the flesh.

153

Cep-stuffed Veal Steaks

SERVES 4

PREPARATION TIME **15 MINUTES**

COOKING TIME **15 MINUTES**

INGREDIENTS

- 4 thick veal steaks
- 2 tbsp butter
- 150 g / 5 ½ oz / 2 cups ceps, sliced
- 1 clove of garlic, crushed
- 2 tbsp flat leaf parsley, chopped
- 2 tbsp crème fraiche
- salt and black pepper

METHOD

1. Preheat the grill to its highest setting and cut a deep pocket into the side of each veal steak with a sharp knife.

2. Heat the butter in a frying pan then fry the ceps for 5 minutes, turning occasionally. Remove from the pan with a slotted spoon and reserve half of them as a garnish. Slice the rest into matchsticks.

3. Add the garlic and parsley to the frying pan and fry for 1 minute, then stir in the crème fraiche and cep matchsticks.

4. Stuff the cep mixture into the veal pockets, season, then grill the steaks for 3 minutes on each side or until cooked to your liking.

5. Transfer the steaks to four warm plates and garnish with the reserved ceps.

TOP TIP
This stuffing also works really well with guinea fowl breasts.

esame
Meatball
asta

VES **4**

PARATION TIME **15 MINUTES**

KING TIME **15 MINUTES**

REDIENTS

g / 8 oz / 1 cup minced lamb
g / 8 oz / 1 cup sausage meat
/ 2 oz / ⅔ cup fresh white breadcrumbs
sp hummus
sp flat leaf parsley, finely chopped
sp sesame seeds
sp olive oil
g / 14 oz / 4 cups dried fusilli
erry tomatoes, quartered
/ 1 ¾ oz / ½ cup Parmesan, finely grated
l leaves to garnish
and black pepper

METHOD

1. Knead the lamb mince, sausage meat, breadcrumbs, hummus and parsley together and season with salt and pepper. Shape the mixture into meatballs and roll in the sesame seeds to coat.

2. Heat half of the oil in a frying pan and fry the meatballs for 15 minutes or until cooked through, turning occasionally.

3. Meanwhile, boil the pasta in salted water according to the packet instructions or until 'al dente'.

4. Drain the pasta, then toss it with the meatballs and tomatoes and dress with the rest of the oil. Divide between four warm bowls and sprinkle generously with Parmesan and basil leaves.

TOP TIP

Try rolling half of the meatballs in poppy seeds for a pretty presentation.

Veal Piccata

SERVES 2

PREPARATION TIME 5 MINUTES

COOKING TIME 10 MINUTES

INGREDIENTS

2 veal escalopes
2 tbsp plain (all-purpose) flour
1 tbsp olive oil
2 tbsp butter
50 ml / 1 ¾ fl. oz / ¼ cup dry white wine
½ lemon
boiled potato batons and halved cherry tomatoes
    to serve
salt and black pepper

METHOD

1. Put a frying pan over a high heat. Season
   veal liberally with salt and pepper, then
   it with flour.

2. Add the olive oil and half the butter to the
   pan. When the butter stops sizzling, low
   in the escalopes. Cook without disturbing
   for 3 minutes, then turn them over and c
   for another 3 minutes. Remove the veal
   the pan and wrap in a double layer of kit
   foil to rest.

3. Add the wine and a squeeze of lemon to
   the pan and reduce until only 2 tbsp of lic
   remains. Whisk in the rest of the butter
   it turns foamy.

4. Serve the veal with potato batons and ch
   tomatoes on the side and spoon over the
   foaming pan juices.

TOP TIP

This recipe also works well with chicken escalopes.

hickpea and omato Salad

METHOD

1. Toss the chickpeas with the cucumber and tomatoes and divide between two bowls.

2. Whisk the oil and lemon juice together with the cumin and a pinch of salt until emulsified, then drizzle it over the salads and serve immediately.

RVES 2

EPARATION TIME 5 MINUTES

GREDIENTS

g / 14 oz / 1 ½ cups canned chickpeas (garbanzo beans), drained

ucumber, peeled and diced

g / 5 ½ oz / 1 cup cherry tomatoes, halved

osp extra virgin olive oil

osp lemon juice

nch of ground cumin

salt

TOP TIP

This also tastes great with butterbeans in place of the chickpeas.

Vegetable Tart

METHOD

1. Preheat the oven to 190°C (170°C fan) / 375F / gas 5.

2. Spoon the hummus into the tart case and arrange the vegetables and chickpeas on top.

3. Transfer the tart to the oven and bake for 20 minutes or until the vegetables are tender and golden brown on top.

SERVES 4

PREPARATION TIME 5 MINUTES

COOKING TIME 20 MINUTES

INGREDIENTS

200 g / 7 oz / ¾ cup hummus
1 savory shortcrust pastry case
4 asparagus spears
1 red onion, sliced
1 courgette (zucchini), sliced
½ red pepper, deseeded and sliced
100 g / 3 ½ oz / ¾ cup preserved artichokes in
    brine, drained and sliced
4 button mushrooms, sliced
2 tbsp canned chickpeas, drained

TOP TIP

Crack an egg into the centre of the tart before baking for a deliciously soft centre.

Roast Guinea Fowl Breast with Asparagus

SERVES 5

PREPARATION TIME 5 MINUTES

COOKING TIME 25 MINUTES

INGREDIENTS

guinea fowl supremes
25 g / 8 oz / 1 cup white asparagus
   spears, trimmed
25 g / 8 oz / 1 cup green asparagus
   spears, trimmed
lemon, juiced and zest finely grated
tbsp runny honey
tbsp tarragon, finely chopped
50 g / 5 ½ oz / ²/₃ cup cold-smoked haddock loin
salad leaves to serve
salt and pepper

METHOD

1. Preheat the oven to 180°C (160°C fan) / 350F / gas 4.

2. Season the guinea fowl supremes well with salt and pepper, then roast them for 25 minutes or until the juices run clear.

3. Meanwhile, steam the asparagus for 6 minutes or until tender.

4. Mix the lemon juice and zest with the honey and tarragon to make a dressing.

5. Roughly chop the haddock with a sharp knife.

6. Serve the guinea fowl with the steamed asparagus on the side. Drizzle over the lemon dressing and top each plate with a few slices of smoked haddock. Garnish with salad leaves.

TOP TIP
Replace the smoked haddock with chunks of pan-fried chorizo.

Penne with Courgette and Lardons

SERVES **4**

PREPARATION TIME **5 MINUTES**

COOKING TIME **12 MINUTES**

INGREDIENTS

400 g / 14 oz / 3 cups dried penne pasta
4 tbsp olive oil
100 g / 2 ⅓ oz / ½ cup lardons
1 large courgette (zucchini), cut into batons
thyme sprigs to garnish
sea salt

METHOD

1. Cook the penne in boiling, salted water according to the packet instructions or until 'al dente'. Drain well.

2. While the pasta is cooking, heat the oil in a frying pan and fry the lardons and courgette batons for 6 minutes or until golden brown.

3. Toss the pasta with the lardons and courgettes, then divide between four warm bowls and garnish with thyme.

TOP TIP
Try replacing the courgette with sugar snap peas.

Vegetable Skewers

SERVES 4

PREPARATION TIME 20 MINUTES

COOKING TIME 8 MINUTES

INGREDIENTS

tbsp olive oil

tbsp cider vinegar

tsp dried herbes de Provence

courgette (zucchini), cut into chunks

cherry tomatoes, halved

button mushrooms, halved

fennel bulb, cut into chunks

salt and black pepper

METHOD

1. Mix the oil with the vinegar, herbs and a pinch of salt and pepper. Pour the mixture over the vegetables and leave to marinate for 15 minutes.

2. Meanwhile, soak 12 wooden skewers in a bowl of cold water.

3. Preheat the grill to its highest setting. Thread the vegetables onto the skewers.

4. Grill the kebabs for 8 minutes, turning occasionally, or until the vegetables are tender and lightly toasted round the edges.

TOP TIP

Try adding chunks of halloumi to the skewers for a great combination of textures.

Pork and Grapefruit Salad

SERVES 4

PREPARATION TIME 15 MINUTES

COOKING TIME 5 MINUTES

INGREDIENTS

2 ruby grapefruit
2 tbsp olive oil
1 pork fillet, sliced
2 handfuls of rocket (arugula)
4 crostini toasts
2 tbsp pine nuts
salt and black pepper

METHOD

1. Slice the top and bottom off the grapefruit. Slice away the peel, then cut out each individual segment, leaving the white pith behind and collecting any juices in a bowl. Discard the pith.

2. Heat the oil in a large frying pan and season the pieces of pork fillet with salt and pepper, then fry them for 1 minute on each side or until just cooked through. Remove the pork from the pan and deglaze with the collected grapefruit juices.

3. Toss the pork with the rocket and grapefruit segments and divide between four plates. Break the crostini into pieces and scatter over the top with the pine nuts. Dress the salads with the pan juices and serve.

TOP TIP

Try using chicken livers instead of the pork for an economical treat.

Desserts

Maraschino Cherry Clafoutis

SERVES 6

PREPARATION TIME 5 MINUTES

COOKING TIME 25 MINUTES

INGREDIENTS

75 g / 2 ½ oz / ⅓ cup butter
75 g / 2 ½ oz / ⅓ cup caster (superfine) sugar
300 ml / 10 ½ fl. oz / 1 ¼ cups whole milk
2 large eggs
50 g / 1 ¾ oz / ⅓ cup plain (all-purpose) flour
2 tbsp ground almonds
200 g / 7 oz / 1 ⅓ cups maraschino cherries,
    drained with stalks intact
pinch of salt

METHOD

1. Preheat the oven to 190°C (170°C fan) / 375F / gas 5.

2. Melt the butter in a saucepan and cook over a low heat until it starts to smell nu Brush a little of the butter around the in of a 20 cm (8 in) diameter quiche dish, th add a spoonful of caster sugar and shak to coat.

3. Whisk together the milk and eggs with t rest of the butter. Sift the flour into a mi bowl with a pinch of salt and stir in the ground almonds and the rest of the suga

4. Make a well in the middle of the dry ingredients and gradually whisk in the li incorporating all the flour from round th outside until you have a lump-free batte

5. Arrange the cherries in the prepared ba dish, pour over the batter and transfer t oven immediately. Bake the clafoutis fo 20–25 minutes or until a skewer inserte in the centre comes out clean.

TOP TIP

Try sprinkling the clafoutis with flaked almonds before baking for added crunch.

peedy
ummer Fruit
rifle

VES 8

PARATION TIME **10 MINUTES**

REDIENTS

g / 10 ½ oz / 2 cups lemon Madeira cake,
liced

p limoncello

/ 1 ¾ oz / ½ cup icing (confectioners') sugar

g / 8 oz / 1 cup Greek yogurt

g / 8 oz / 1 cup mascarpone

g / 7 oz / 1 ⅓ cups raspberries

g / 7 oz / 1 ⅓ cups blueberries

METHOD

1. Lay half of the cake slices in a trifle bowl
   and sprinkle with half of the limoncello.

2. Fold the icing sugar into the yogurt and
   mascarpone, then spoon half of it over
   the cake.

3. Top with half of the berries, then cover
   with the rest of the cake and limoncello.
   Spoon the rest of the yogurt mixture on
   top and scatter over the rest of the berries.

4. Serve straight away or leave for 20 minutes
   for the flavours to infuse.

TOP TIP

Add the grated zest of
an orange and lemon to
the mascarpone
mixture.

DESSERTS

Sweet Bagel Sandwich

METHOD

1. Toast the bagel, then spread the bottom half with lemon curd.

2. Arrange the strawberry slices and raspberries on top, then sprinkle with lime zest, garnish with mint and serve immediately.

SERVES 1

PREPARATION TIME 3 MINUTES

COOKING TIME 2 MINUTES

INGREDIENTS

1 sugar-topped bagel, split in half
1 tbsp lemon curd
1 large strawberry, sliced
4 raspberries
½ tsp lime zest, finely grated
a small sprig of mint

TOP TIP

Top the fruit with a spoonful of whipped cream for extra decadence.

Speedy Raspberry and Almond Rice Puddings

SERVES 6

PREPARATION TIME **15 MINUTES**

COOKING TIME **10 MINUTES**

INGREDIENTS

100 g / 4 oz / ½ cup short grain rice
75 g / 2 ½ oz / ¼ cup runny honey
1 litres / 2 pints / 4 ½ cups almond milk
200 g / 9 oz / 1 ⅔ cups raspberries
25 g / 1 oz / ⅓ cup flaked (slivered) almonds

METHOD

1. Preheat the oven to 140°C (120°C fan) / 275F / gas 1.

2. Stir the rice and honey into the almond milk in a microwavable bowl, then cover with cling film and pierce the top.

3. Cook on high for 5 minutes, then stir well and cook for another 5 minutes or until all the milk has been absorbed and the rice is tender. Leave to stand for 5 minutes.

4. Crush half of the raspberries with a fork, then stir the purée into the rice with the whole berries, reserving a few to garnish.

5. Divide the rice pudding between six glasses and sprinkle the almonds and reserved raspberries over the top.

TOP TIP
The rice puddings are also delicious served chilled if you make them in advance.

Blackberry and Apple Compote with Meringue Topping

SERVES 6

PREPARATION TIME **15 MINUTES**

COOKING TIME **15 MINUTES**

INGREDIENTS

2 Bramley apples, peeled, cored and chopped
200 g / 7 oz / 1 ⅓ cups blackberries
50 g / 1 ¾ oz / ¼ cup granulated sugar
4 large egg whites
110 g / 4 oz / 1 cup caster (superfine) sugar

METHOD

1. Put the apples, blackberries and granulated sugar in a saucepan with a splash of water. Cover the pan and cook over a medium heat for 10 minutes, stirring occasionally until the fruit has reduced to a thick compote. Spoon into six glasses.

2. Whisk the egg whites until stiff, then gradually whisk in half the sugar until the mixture is very shiny. Fold in the remaining sugar with a large metal spoon.

3. Spoon the meringue into a piping bag fitted with a large star nozzle and pipe a swirl on top of the compote in each glass.

4. Toast under a hot grill for 3–4 minutes or until golden brown. Serve immediately.

TOP TIP

Crumble some sponge cake into the bottom of each glass first.

hocolate and Hazelnut Brownies

MKES **16**

PREPARATION TIME **5 MINUTES**

COOKING TIME **25 MINUTES**

INGREDIENTS

g / 4 oz / ½ cup dark chocolate (minimum
70% cocoa solids), chopped
g / 3 oz / ¾ cup unsweetened cocoa
powder, sifted
g / 8 oz / 1 cup butter
g / 1 lb / 2 ½ cups light brown sugar
rge eggs
g / 4 oz / 1 cup self-raising flour
g / 2 ½ oz / ½ cup toasted hazelnuts
(cobnuts), chopped

METHOD

1. Preheat the oven to 160°C (140°C fan) / 325F / gas 3 and oil and line a 20 cm x 20 cm (8 in x 8 in) square cake tin.

2. Melt the chocolate, cocoa and butter in a saucepan, then leave to cool a little.

3. Whisk the sugar and eggs together with an electric whisk for 3 minutes or until very light and creamy.

4. Pour in the chocolate mixture and sift over the flour. Reserve 1 tbsp of the nuts to decorate and fold the rest into the brownie batter.

5. Scrape into the prepared tin and bake for 25 minutes or until the outside is set, but the centre is still quite soft.

6. Leave the brownie to cool completely, then cut into 12 squares and sprinkle with the reserved hazelnuts.

TOP TIP
Try adding the grated zest of an orange when you melt the butter.

Ginger Nuts

MAKES **36**

PREPARATION TIME **10 MINUTES**

COOKING TIME **15 MINUTES**

INGREDIENTS

75 g / 2 ½ oz / ⅓ cup butter, softened
100 g / 3 ½ oz / ⅓ cup golden syrup
225 g / 8 oz / 1 ½ cups self-raising flour
100 g / 3 ½ oz / ½ cup caster (superfine) sugar
2 tsp ground ginger
1 large egg, beaten

METHOD

1. Preheat the oven to 180°C (160°C fan)
   / 355F / gas 4 and line 2 baking trays with
   greaseproof paper.

2. Melt the butter and golden syrup together
   in a saucepan. Mix the flour, sugar and
   ground ginger together, then stir in the
   melted butter mixture and the beaten egg

3. Use a teaspoon to portion the mixture onto
   the baking trays, leaving plenty of room for
   the biscuits to spread.

4. Bake for 15 minutes or until golden brown.
   Transfer the biscuits to a wire rack and
   leave to cool and harden.

TOP TIP

Replace the ground ginger with ground cinnamon for a sweet and spicy treat.

Roasted Pineapple

SERVES 4

PREPARATION TIME 5 MINUTES

COOKING TIME 25 MINUTES

INGREDIENTS

pineapple, peeled and cored
200 g / 7 oz / ¾ cup caster (superfine) sugar
cinnamon stick
cardamom pods
star anise
piece orange peel
amaretti biscuits, crushed
scoops vanilla ice cream
bsp crème fraiche
caramel shards, mint leaves and plum slices
to garnish

METHOD

1. Preheat the oven to 200°C (180°C fan) / 400F / gas 6 and cut the pineapple into even-sized batons.

2. Put the sugar, spices and orange peel in a saucepan with 300 ml / ½ pint / 1 ¼ cups of water and stir over a medium heat to dissolve the sugar. Once the sugar has dissolved, stop stirring and let it boil for 8 minutes or until thick and syrupy. Strain it into a jug to remove the spices.

3. Arrange the pineapple in a roasting tin in a single layer, then pour three quarters of the spiced syrup over the pineapple. Roast for 15 minutes, turning the pieces over halfway through.

4. Arrange the pineapple batons on four plates, then add a spoonful of crushed amaretti and top with a scoop of ice cream.

5. Spoon the crème fraiche around the plate, then garnish with caramel shards, mint leaves and plum slices.

TOP TIP
Serve with coconut ice cream and a drizzle of chocolate sauce.

Apple and Amaretti Verrines

SERVES 4

PREPARATION TIME 5 MINUTES

INGREDIENTS

50 g / 1 ¾ oz / ½ cup icing (confectioners')
  sugar, sieved
450 g / 1 lb / 2 cups Greek yogurt
50 g / 1 ¾ oz / ½ cup apple compote
100 g / 3 ½ oz / 2 cups amaretti biscuits, crushed
4 tbsp amaretto liqueur

METHOD

1. Stir the icing sugar into the yogurt.

2. Fold the apple compote into the crushed biscuits and divide half of the mixture between four glasses. Drizzle with half of the liqueur.

3. Spoon over half of the yogurt, then top with the rest of the compote mixture and drizzle with the rest of the liqueur.

4. Top with the rest of the yogurt and serve immediately.

TOP TIP

Try replacing the apple with peaches when they're in season.

hocolate nd Walnut rownie Cake

VES 8

PARATION TIME 5 MINUTES

KING TIME 25 MINUTES

GREDIENTS

g / 4 oz / ½ cup dark chocolate (minimum 70%
cocoa solids), chopped
/ 3 oz / ¾ cup unsweetened cocoa
powder, sifted
g / 8 oz / 1 cup butter
g / 1 lb / 2 ½ cups light brown sugar
rge eggs
g / 4 oz / 1 cup self-raising flour
/ 2 ½ oz / ½ cup walnuts, finely chopped

METHOD

1. Preheat the oven to 160°C (140°C fan)
   / 325F / gas 3 and oil and line a 23 cm (9 in)
   round cake tin with greaseproof paper.

2. Melt the chocolate, cocoa and butter together
   in a saucepan, then leave to cool a little.

3. Whisk the sugar and eggs together with an
   electric whisk for 3 minutes or until very
   light and creamy.

4. Pour in the chocolate mixture and sieve over
   the flour, then fold everything together with
   the walnuts.

5. Scrape the mixture into the tin and bake for
   25 minutes or until the outside is set, but the
   centre is still quite soft.

6. Leave the brownie to cool completely before
   cutting into wedges and serving.

TOP TIP

Replace the walnuts
with chopped salted
peanuts for a more
salty flavour.

193

Apple Tart

SERVES **4**

PREPARATION TIME **10 MINUTES**

COOKING TIME **20 MINUTES**

INGREDIENTS

400 g / 14 oz / 1 ⅓ cups ready-to-roll puff pastry
3 tbsp apricot jam (jelly)
2 apples, peeled, cored and sliced

METHOD

1. Preheat the oven to 220°C (200°C fan) / 425F / gas 7.

2. Roll out the pastry into a long, narrow rectangle on a lightly floured surface. Transfer the pastry to a non-stick baking tray.

3. Spread the top of the pastry with apricot jam, leaving a 1 cm (½ in) border around the outside. Arrange the apple slices on top in a single layer.

4. Transfer the baking tray to the oven and bake for 20 minutes or until the pastry is cooked through underneath.

TOP TIP

This recipe is also delicious made with pears or plums.

Raspberry and Nut Yogurt Pots

METHOD

1. Stir the honey into the yogurt and divide between four glasses.

2. Decorate the yogurt with the raspberries, pistachios and pine nuts, then drizzle with balsamic vinegar.

ERVES 4

REPARATION TIME 5 MINUTES

INGREDIENTS

bsp runny honey
50 g / 1 lb / 2 cups Greek yogurt
raspberries
bsp pistachio nuts, roughly chopped
bsp pine nuts
sp balsamic vinegar

TOP TIP

This recipe is also delicious made with blueberries in place of the raspberries.

DESSERTS

Strawberry and Raspberry Mousse

SERVES 4

PREPARATION TIME **30 MINUTES**

INGREDIENTS

150 g / 5 ½ oz / 1 cup strawberries, quartered
150 g / 5 ½ oz / 1 cup raspberries
4 tbsp caster (superfine) sugar
175 ml / 6 fl. oz / ⅔ cup canned evaporated
   milk, chilled
225 g / 8 oz / 1 cup Greek yogurt

METHOD

1. Reserve a few of the strawberries and raspberries for decoration and put the rest in a liquidizer with the sugar.

2. Blend until smooth, then pass the mixture through a sieve to remove the seeds.

3. Whip the evaporated milk with an electric whisk for about 6 minutes or until doubled in volume.

4. Fold in the fruit purée and yogurt, then spoon into four glasses and chill for 20 minutes.

5. Top with the reserved fruit and serve immediately.

TOP TIP
This recipe also works really well with blueberries and blackberries.

Marinated Summer Berries

SERVES 6

PREPARATION TIME 30 MINUTES

INGREDIENTS

150 g / 5 ½ oz / 1 cup strawberries, halved
150 g / 5 ½ oz / 1 cup raspberries
150 g / 5 ½ oz / 1 cup blackberries
150 g / 5 ½ oz / 1 cup blueberries
2 tbsp caster (superfine) sugar
1 tbsp mint, roughly chopped
2 limes, juiced

METHOD

1. Mix all of the ingredients together and leave to marinate for 30 minutes.

2. Spoon into six small bowls and serve immediately.

TOP TIP

Try adding 4 tbsp of crème de cassis to the marinade.

Apricot and Almond Puddings

SERVES **4**

PREPARATION TIME **10 MINUTES**

COOKING TIME **20 MINUTES**

INGREDIENTS

55 g / 2 oz / ½ cup ground almonds
55 g / 2 oz / ¼ cup caster (superfine) sugar
55 g / 2 oz / ¼ cup butter, softened
1 large egg
1 tsp almond essence
4 canned apricot halves
1 tbsp granulated sugar
2 tbsp flaked (slivered) almonds
lemon thyme to garnish

METHOD

1. Preheat the oven to 200°C (180°C fan) / 400F / gas 6.

2. Combine the ground almonds, sugar, butter, egg and almond essence in a bowl and whisk together for 2 minutes or until completely smooth.

3. Spoon the mixture into four individual baking dishes, then top each one with an apricot half and sprinkle with granulated sugar.

4. Bake the puddings for 20 minutes, then garnish with flaked almonds and lemon thyme.

TOP TIP

Try using canned pears in place of the apricots.

Crêpes with Chocolate Dipping Sauce

ERVES 4

REPARATION TIME **10 MINUTES**

OOKING TIME **20 MINUTES**

NGREDIENTS

0 g / 5 ½ oz / 1 cup plain (all-purpose) flour

arge egg

25 ml / 11 ½ fl. oz / 1 ⅓ cups whole milk

bsp butter

or the dipping sauce

0 ml / 3 ½ fl. oz / 1 ½ cups double (heavy)
    cream

bsp brandy

0 g / 3 ½ oz / ½ cup dark chocolate (minimum
    60 % cocoa solids), chopped

METHOD

1. To make the dipping sauce, heat the cream and brandy to simmering point, then pour it over the chocolate and stir to emulsify. Spoon into four serving bowls.

2. Sieve the flour into a bowl and make a well in the centre. Break in the egg and pour in the milk, then use a whisk to gradually incorporate all of the flour from round the outside.

3. Melt the butter in a small frying pan, then whisk it into the batter.

4. Put the buttered frying pan back over a low heat. Add a small ladle of batter and swirl the pan to coat the bottom.

5. When it starts to dry and curl up at the edges, turn the pancake over with a spatula and cook the other side until golden brown and cooked through.

6. Repeat with the rest of the mixture, then serve the crêpes with the dipping sauce.

TOP TIP

Serve the crêpes with vanilla ice cream for a great hot and cold combination.

205

Marinated Strawberry and Lemon Verrines

SERVES 4

PREPARATION TIME 30 MINUTES

INGREDIENTS

4 tbsp white balsamic vinegar
200 g / 7 oz / 1 ⅓ cups strawberries, sliced
1 lemon
50 g / 1 ¾ oz / ½ cup icing (confectioners') sugar
225 g / 8 oz / 1 cup Greek yogurt
225 g / 8 oz / 1 cup whipped cream

METHOD

1. Pour the balsamic vinegar over the strawberries and leave to marinate for 25 minutes.

2. Use a citrus zester to finely pare the lemon ring into strips and reserve for the garnish. Squeeze the lemon and mix the juice with the icing sugar to dissolve, then stir it into the yogurt. Fold in the whipped cream.

3. Divide the yogurt mixture between four glasses and top with the marinated strawberries. Sprinkle with lemon zest and serve immediately.

TOP TIP

Replace the balsamic vinegar with orange liqueur for an adults-only treat.

Spiced Fruit Salad

SERVES 4

PREPARATION TIME **20 MINUTES**

COOKING TIME **10 MINUTES**

INGREDIENTS

10 g / 7 oz / ¾ cup caster (superfine) sugar
cinnamon stick
star anise
pomegranate, halved
pineapple, peeled and cut into chunks
pears, peeled, cored and cut into chunks
0 g / 5 ½ oz / 1 cup seedless red grapes

METHOD

1. Put the sugar and spices in a saucepan with 300 ml / ½ pint / 1 ¼ cups of water and stir over a medium heat to dissolve the sugar. Once the sugar has dissolved, stop stirring and let it boil for 8 minutes or until thick and syrupy.

2. Hold the pomegranate halves over the pan and hit the backs with a wooden spoon to release the seeds. Stir them into the syrup with the rest of the fruit, then leave to cool and infuse for 20 minutes.

TOP TIP

Cinnamon ice cream makes a great accompaniment to this fruit salad.

209

DESSERTS

Poached Apricots with Honey and Rosemary

SERVES 4

PREPARATION TIME 5 MINUTES

COOKING TIME 5 MINUTES

INGREDIENTS

12 apricots, halved and stoned
100 ml / 3 ½ fl. oz / ½ cup apple juice
4 tbsp runny honey
1 tbsp rosemary leaves

METHOD

1. Put the apricots in a saucepan with the apple juice, honey and rosemary.

2. Cover and simmer gently for 5 minutes or until the apricots are soft, but still holding their shape. Serve warm or leave to cool before chilling.

TOP TIP
This recipe also works really well with peaches in place of the apricots.

hocolate nd Walnut ancakes

VES **4**

PARATION TIME **5 MINUTES**

KING TIME **20 MINUTES**

REDIENTS

g / 7 oz / 1 ⅓ cups plain (all-purpose) flour
/ 1 ¾ oz / ½ cup unsweetened cocoa powder
baking powder
ge eggs
ml / 10 ½ fl. oz / 1 ¼ cups milk
sp butter
sp walnuts, chopped

METHOD

1. Mix the flour, cocoa and baking powder
   in a bowl and make a well in the centre.
   Break in the eggs and pour in the milk,
   then use a whisk to gradually incorporate
   all of the flour from round the outside.

2. Divide the butter between four mini frying
   pans and heat to melt, then whisk the butter
   into the batter. Put the buttered frying pans
   back over a low heat.

3. Spoon the batter into the pans and cook for
   2 minutes or until small bubbles start to
   appear on the surface. Turn the pancakes
   over with a spatula and cook the other side
   until golden brown and cooked through.

4. Repeat until all the batter has been used,
   keeping the finished batches warm in a low
   oven. Pile the pancakes onto warm plates
   and sprinkle with walnuts.

TOP TIP
Spread the pancakes
with chocolate spread
and sprinkle with
nuts.

Baked Apples

SERVES 4

PREPARATION TIME 5 MINUTES

COOKING TIME 25 MINUTES

INGREDIENTS

4 small Bramley apples
4 tbsp salted butter
4 tbsp light brown sugar

METHOD

1. Preheat the oven to 180°C (160°C fan) / 355F / gas 4.

2. Use an apple corer to remove the apple cores, then sit them in a snug baking dish. Beat the butter and sugar together then pack the mixture into the cavities.

3. Bake the apples for 25 minutes or until a skewer will slide in easily all the way to the centre.

TOP TIP

Serve the apples with a scoop of caramel ice cream for extra indulgence.

Portuguese Custard Tarts

KES **12**

EPARATION TIME **10 MINUTES**

OKING TIME **20 MINUTES**

GREDIENTS

g pack of ready-rolled, all-butter puff pastry
rge egg yolks, beaten
g / 1 ¾ oz / ¼ cup caster (superfine) sugar
p cornflour (cornstarch)
ml / 8 fl. oz / ¾ cup whole milk
emon, zest finely grated
sp ground cinnamon

METHOD

1. Preheat the oven to 200°C (180°C fan) / 390F / gas 6.

2. Unroll the pastry on a floured surface and cut out 12 circles with a pastry cutter.

3. Use the circles to line a 12-hole cupcake tin.

4. Mix the rest of the ingredients together in a jug, then pour it into the pastry cases.

5. Transfer the tin to the oven and bake for 20 minutes or until the pastry is golden brown and cooked through underneath.

TOP TIP

Serve the tarts with vanilla-flavoured whipped cream.

Orange and Passion Fruit Verrines

SERVES 4

PREPARATION TIME 30 MINUTES

INGREDIENTS

2 oranges
50 g / 1 ¾ oz / ½ cup icing (confectioners') sugar, sieved
450 g / 1 lb / 2 cups Greek yogurt
4 passion fruit
150 g / 5 ½ oz / ⅔ cup coconut cake, cubed

METHOD

1. Use a vegetable peeler to pare 4 thin slices of orange zest and reserve for decoration. Slice the top and bottom off the oranges. Slice away the peel then cut out each individual segment, leaving the white pith behind. Discard the pith.

2. Fold the icing sugar into the yogurt.

3. Divide the orange segments between four glass bowls and top with the pulp and seeds from 2 of the passion fruit. Spoon over half of the yogurt.

4. Arrange the cake cubes on top, then spoon over the rest of the yogurt and top with the rest of the passion fruit pulp. Garnish with the reserved orange zest.

TOP TIP

Replace the oranges with ruby grapefruit for a sharper flavour.

Index